D1145880

VANESSA
The Werewolf Hairdresser

For Skevoula, my hairdresser
J.W.

For the Godlieb Family, Klub Barbounia members
K.P.

www.korkypaul.com

ORCHARD BOOKS
96 Leonard Street, London EC2A 4XD
Orchard Books Australia
32/45-51 Huntley Street, Alexandria, NSW 2015
ISBN 1 84362 156 8 (hardback)
ISBN 1 84362 148 7 (paperback)
First published in Great Britain in 2004
First paperback publication in 2005
Text © Jeanne Willis 2004
Illustrations © Korky Paul 2004
A CIP catalogue record for this book is available
from the British Library.
1 3 5 7 9 10 8 6 4 2 (hardback)
1 3 5 7 9 10 8 6 4 2 (paperback)
Printed in Great Britain

VANESSA
The Werewolf Hairdresser

Jeanne Willis * Korky Paul

ORCHARD BOOKS

VANESSA

The Werewolf Hairdresser

Come in, love, please take a chair.
Just got to perm Rapunzel's hair.
Guess what I found in the final rinse?
Only a bloomin' handsome prince!

He'd been driving her up the wall.
"Let down your hair!" and up he'd crawl.
I said she should go for a nice, short crop,
Or a little bob. That'd make him stop!

Have a magazine. You'll have to wait.

My last appointment ran on late.

I had the ugly sisters of Cinderella,

Wanting to impress the same poor fella.

Believe you me, they took a while.

They bought in a piccy of a favourite style.

They wanted hair like a Barbie Doll's.

I tried, but they both went out like trolls.

Here's some goss! You know Snow White?
Her hair's not black, it's really light.
It's mostly grey, not ebony.
I tint it for her, regularly.

Goldilocks is mousy-brown.

She comes in here when she's in town.

She thinks that blondes have much more fun —

They do with bears, ask anyone!

Peter Pan's come here for years.
I trim his nostril hair and ears.
He plays around. I'm sick of it,
I wish he would grow up a bit.

He must be ninety. Even so,
His wig's that good, you'd never know!
(Though strictly, between you and me,
He's had some plastic surgery.)

I used to run this place alone –
I swept the floor and manned the phone,
Until it all became too much.
Thank goodness Beryl got in touch.

Beryl used to live next-door.
We've been friends since we were four.
We practised hairstyles on her cat,
And manicured my brother's rat.

We both grew up and worked in salons –
I did blow-dries, she did talons.
Then I bought my own place, see?
And Beryl came to work for me.

Now I do hair and she does beauty.
We both take turns on reception duty,
And if there's a problem, I'll refer
My awkward clients on to her.

Father Christmas, would you believe,
Always wants a trim on Christmas Eve?
It's our busiest time, but he gets his way
Or we don't get presents on Christmas Day.

As for Beauty and her mate, the Beast,
You'd think he'd leave a tip at least.
We gave him a make-over. Worked 'til late
But all he said was, "My fringe isn't straight!"

Most of our clients are really sweet.
Beryl pedicures the giant's feet.
There's a lot of call for the tanning bed –
It's booked right up with the Living Dead.

There was one bloke who came in late —
We won't forget him, what a state!
He wanted me to cut his hair.
Beryl called, "Vanessa? It's Mr Were."

I was out the back with a cup of tea.
I'd finished for the day, you see.
I'd been on my feet all afternoon.
It was dark outside. No stars, full moon.

Well, Mr Were seemed very down.
I put him in a plastic gown.
"Cheer up!" I said. "You misery,
It might never happen." Silly me!

I asked if he'd booked a holiday,
But he said he never went away,
He always haunted the same old place.
Then he asked me to trim his hairy face.

The more I trimmed, the more it grew —
I said, "Do hormones trouble you?"
He only answered with a growl,
And started chewing on a towel.

Beryl and I began to stare,
~~For~~ he was sprouting thick, black hair.
And then his eyes began to change –
He really did look very strange.

He seemed to grow enormous paws.
He walked about upon all fours.
His eyes were glistening and red.
"This look is *so* not you," I said.

"Those eyebrows need a pluck, they do!
Here, Beryl will look after you,
She does a lovely body wax.
Come out the back. Lie down. Relax."

Oh, men make such an awful fuss.

They are not used to pain like us.

When Beryl got her wax strips out,

You should have heard him scream and shout.

He showed his fangs and dribbled gore.
"Oh dear," said Beryl. "Was it sore?
We'll do your toenails now, I think.
Which colour polish? Peach or pink?"

"Flesh!" he howled. "That's what I need!"
But Beryl bravely disagreed
And served him cups of camomile
With biscuits and a charming smile.

He wolfed it down, but even so
He sniffed around and wouldn't go.
He cornered Beryl by the sink
And said he needed blood to drink.

I thought he'd eat her whole, or worse,
And so I said, "I'll get my purse.
The corner shop won't shut 'til late.
I'll buy some blood from there, old mate."

"Meanwhile, Sir, please take a seat
Inside our Sauna Room. The heat
Is very pleasant, you will find.
You're shy? We'll lock it from behind.

"Just call us when you've had enough.
Here's some soap and shower stuff.
Just slip your things off. In you go!
We'll see you in an hour or so."

I locked him in and off we went
To Sharon's hen night down in Kent.
We had such fun, I have to say
We forgot about him, until next day.

We opened the sauna. There he sat
As smooth as a baby's bum at that!
And sweet and gentle as a child.
"I feel quite human now!" he smiled.

He left and said, "I'll be back soon.
Can you fit me in for the next full moon?"
I said, "We're booked-up, I'm afraid...
Try the Poodle Parlour in Town Parade!"

Written by Jeanne Willis * Illustrated by Korky Paul

Jeff the Witch's Chef	1 84362 146 0
Lillibet the Monster Vet	1 84362 145 2
Norman the Demon Doorman	1 84362 159 2
Vanessa the Werewolf Hairdresser	1 84362 148 7
Annie the Gorilla Nanny	1 84362 155 X
Gabby the Vampire Cabbie	1 84362 158 4
Bert the Fairies' Fashion Expert	1 84362 149 5
Iddy Bogey, the Ogre Yogi	1 84362 160 6

All priced at £3.99 each